THE
MADISON AVENUE
SPEECH BOOK

Also by
Alan Koehler:

The Madison Avenue
Cook Book
for people who can't
cook and don't want
other people to know it

McGraw-Hill Book Company
New York   Toronto   London

THE
MADISON AVENUE
SPEECH BOOK

FOR

PEOPLE

WHO

ARE

SCARED

TO

MAKE

A SPEECH

AND DON'T WANT TO SHOW IT

BY ALAN KOEHLER

THE MADISON AVENUE SPEECH BOOK

"Song of the Vagabonds": lyrics by BRIAN
HOOKER, music by Rudolf Friml. Copyright © 1925 by Famous Music Corporation. Copyright renewed 1952 and assigned
to Famous Music Corporation.

cooking can be for kicks,
but speaking is somehow for keeps
                    —G. K. CHESTERTON

Contents

THE
MADISON AVENUE
SPEECH BOOK

nobody who wants to rise in a Madison Avenue advertising agency can just silently sit there, with his childhood scars peeping through his crewcut. Advertising is an articulate business. To get ahead, you have to prove that you are articulate too. You have to get up and make a presentation to clients or fellow executives from time to time. You have to do this even if you're deathly afraid of public speaking. Anyone who is afraid of public speaking automatically wants to conceal his fright. People expect murderers to approach the electric chair, and speakers the microphone, fearlessly. But on Madison Avenue there is a vital reason for a speaker to conceal his fear. For the least smell of it may fatally attract the interest of the man-eating sharks ubiquitous in Madison Avenue waters.

This book is called *The Madison Avenue Speech Book* because it tells you how to appear to be a pillar of poise while making a speech, when actually you're frozen with fear. Do not let the simplicity, nor what some may interpret as the slickness, of our advice distract you from its soundness. Do not let any of the particular illustrative examples we may use mislead you into thinking that this is a private little paper for fey or recherché types . . . certainly, you may feel thankfully, not including you.

Nay, this book is, and these principles work, for *anybody* who is terrified to give a speech— from the parent confronted with talking to the

PTA on elementary school toilet facilities, in-adequacy of, to the apparently polished politician, outwardly cool as his carnation, but inwardly (and there are many) sore afraid. Further, the Madison Avenue technique works whether you do or don't think you have anything to say, whether you're galvanized with conviction or dissolved by lack of it, whether you covet the spotlight or just want to get it off your back, whether you wish to seem dead serious or lighthearted, and whether the stakes are high or low.

The secret of Madison Avenue speaking is to keep the audience so absorbed, diverted, preoccupied or entertained that it doesn't have much chance to notice the speaker's terror, which slithers past undetected. And to keep the speaker, aware that he is doing well, from producing so much terror to detect. Miraculously, what is planned primarily as a camouflage for panic on the podium almost invariably turns out to be a successful speech. And while successful speeches that aren't Madison Avenue speeches are given every day, *Madison Avenue-ifying any speech makes it better than it would have been.* This is why many canny speakers who aren't frightened at all give nothing but Madison Avenue speeches.

Let us recall, before we go on, that people are the animals most capable of boring each other simply because they're the only ones that talk. And that no kind of talking can have a higher-caliber bore than public talking. Everybody has sat through his share of speeches that have made him wish that not freedom of, but from, speech had been included in the Bill of Rights. While public speaking authorities itemize all kinds of speeches, there are indeed but two kinds: boring ones and nonboring ones. And nobody thinks the same of a speaker after a talk as before, but always worse or better, according to the kind he gives.

Conventional speakers make the error of conceiving a speech like the decline and fall of the Roman Empire—as a lengthy discourse on a single subject, with an Aristotelian beginning, a middle, and (only at last) an end. Yet they seem rarely able to come up with enough speechworthy material on this single subject to sustain interest through an entire speech. The audience grows bored, free to focus its attention more upon speaker than speech, and to seize upon anything interesting to occupy its mind . . . than which there's no tenant so fascinating as a speaker's nervousness. The nervous speaker, sensing this, simply produces still more nervous symptoms for his audience to observe.

Unlike the conventional speaker, who risks boring his audience by ladling an entire speech from a single pot, the Madison Avenue speaker keeps attention keen by serving up his speech in *courses*—e.g., appetizer, soup, fish, meat, vegetable, salad, dessert and coffee, and maybe even a pousse-café—and by attractively *garnishing* each course. Reduced to its essence, his technique seems so simple that we're all but embarrassed to reduce it. Really all he does to his speech—or, as it may turn out, his *divertissement*—is:

 **split it up**

Instead of attempting to sustain a single subject, he divides his speech into *parts,* and draws upon a variety of *different* subjects, one for each part. *Each subject need have no more in common with its fellows than interest for the particular audience.* Naturally, half a dozen short different parts, disconnected except for a ribbon of relevancy for the audience, fall far more lightly on the ear than would one long same connected whole. And, just as merely being served in succession on the same table transforms diverse dishes into a meal, merely being spoken by the same speaker makes his various parts "cohee" as a speech. (Yet the speech remains, if we may mix our metaphor, composed of watertight compartments like the *Queen Mary:* each an autonomous little speechette likely to survive any mishap that might befall another.)

We will first discuss split-it-up, and then dress-it-up, observing that a Madison Avenue speech is the easiest of all possible speeches to prepare as well as to give. For—to give our metaphor another whirl in the Mixmaster—there is a minimum of polishing necessary to achieve the professional sparkle characteristic of one. In fact, this sparkle may derive more from the mere *variety* and *brevity* of the various parts, and the accessories with which they're decorated, than even their content.

split it up

Slick—and backwards—though it may seem, the Madison Avenue speaker begins his preparation by determining how long must it all go on . . . that is, how short dare his speech be. (He marvels that speakers typically struggle to make their speeches longer, when they should be struggling to make them shorter; shorter speeches are not only generically superior to longer ones, but obviously provide a speaker less opportunity to betray himself.) The length of his speech determines the number of parts he needs to fill it. He needs a different part, on the average, for every three minutes of talking time. Hence, a 10-minute talk requires three parts, a 15-minute talk five parts. Already the chore seems easier. You face a series of little surmountable hurdles, instead of one enormous insurmountable one.

Then list all the subjects you are (or could conveniently become) able to talk interestingly about that are of specific concern to the meeting you'll address. Give yourself a little time to think—you need as many good subjects as you have parts. You needn't reject a germane subject because you have only a few things worth saying about it; your parts are so short you haven't *room* to say more than a few things about it. You'll notice that the eclectic Madison Avenue format allows you to *use* many more of the things worth saying you *do* think of. And that having to compress subjects into little parts discourages you from talking on subjects too sweeping to be interesting. The more pinpointed any subject, the more likely its success:

a *Yellowstone Park* part hasn't so good a chance as a *Bears in Yellowstone Park* part.

Then begin jotting down on a note pad, as a stream of consciousness, every snatch of thought occurring to you that usefully applies to these subjects. Keep pencil and paper beside bed and bath—the best thoughts wait to strike till times you're sure to forget them. Keep your eyes open and, just because you're looking for material, you'll find it; you're suddenly like a pregnant woman who begins noticing all the other pregnant women. Cull what you can from anything you read. Bend any intelligent conversation you dare to a discussion of what you will say. Put off cronies and, instead, lunch, drink and dine with interesting people to squeeze ideas out of them. Only when all the accessible wells are dry should the writing begin.

But perhaps an incidental word of caution here. Remember that all opinions, theories, recommendations, postulations and conclusions de-

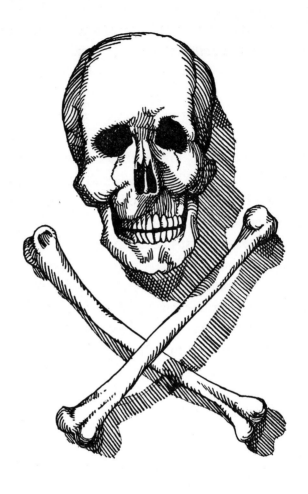

mand the support of concrete *facts* or *examples,* failure to supply & apply which can be fatal.

We say the *writing* may now begin because, while some speakers talk well enough extemporaneously, the Madison Avenue speaker feels he'll be better if he writes his speech word for word. He reasons that anybody would rather hear *A Midsummer Night's Dream* as written than as played by players exposed to merely a synopsis of the plot, who made up their lines as they went along. On Madison Avenue people usually write even their ad libs. But your speech actually all but writes itself: parts are so short that filling them up can be little more than editing and fitting together your stream of consciousness items. They're so short that you need use only the cream of your material. They're so short that there's little chance to get complicated or tangled up in them.

We see the Madison Avenue split-it-up technique at work on an actual speech in the following:

case history

Jonathan Loose, of Foote, Loose & Fancy, management consultants, reacted to the invitation to address the Memphis Junior Chamber of Commerce with what could only be described as total recoil.

The suggested subject—"Memphis: Miracle of the Mississippi"—left him damp with despair. Besides, all his life he had dreaded any speaking more public than asking the stewardess for a pillow. He agreed to make the talk only because the audience would be larded with potential clients for FL&F, which could use them.

Loose had little faith in the Madison Avenue, or any, public speaking method. He believed that the skill of public speaking counselors went into making their advice sound easy, when actually it was supremely difficult, to follow.

But of all the unworkable procedures to use in preparing a speech, the Madison Avenue was the least unattractive because of the results it promised. The trouble with it was that several good subjects for a speech surely must be harder to think of than a single good one. Anyway, he didn't see how he had much choice, since there he was with a subject already assigned him.

His treasure at the typewriter, Miss Jacobus, took not so dim a view. She liked to go to lectures. She had noticed that few successful professional speakers seemed bound by the limits of their announced subject, unless this subject happened to be a very general one.

These speakers would stick only to subjects like "How To Be a Fashion Plate on a Budget," which allowed them the latitude to split their speech up into parts, and to say almost anything interesting about an entire field they could think of.

But when they were coping with a constricting subject like "Memphis: Miracle of the Mississippi," they touched on it only lightly and filled their speech with other, albeit related, matters. No one seemed to care. Or even notice.

Miss Jacobus was confident, also, that lurking in Loose's mind were enough good subjects for the speech at hand. She volunteered to help flush them.

"Perhaps you have some thoughts on how Memphis could become even more of a miracle of the Mississippi than it presently is," she said, to get things started.

"I'm afraid they're all pretty obvious," he replied.

"But don't you find that it's often the obvious that's sadly overlooked?" she murmured.

"You happen to be quoting *me*, Miss Jacobus. I've always said that *nothing* requires constant re-examination so much as the obvious."

Miss Jacobus wrote that down. "Go on," she said.

"Well, obviously, Memphis like almost any big city could use a lot more trees and a lot fewer billboards."

"OK. What else?"

"I know," Loose continued lamely after a long pause, "how Fort Lauderdale went about solving what was, I admit, an entirely dissimilar set of problems from the one confronting Memphis." Miss Jacobus made a note of that too.

"Have *we* ever assisted in a civic project?" she asked.

26

"I wish we had, because that might help make Memphis itself want to hire us, but alas we have not," Loose replied, but Miss Jacobus, after a moment's hesitation, made another note.

"Apropos nothing," he finally went on after another long pause, "something that irritates me is the way nobody wants to do what they're paid to do any more. Salesmen don't sell, promoters don't promote, executives don't execute. And yet everybody expects instant gravy train." Here Miss Jacobus' pencil fairly flew.

This kind of rambling exchange continued between them off and on through the afternoon.

At one point Loose delivered a far from eloquent soliloquy on how, while a committee couldn't have flown the Atlantic, disagreement within itself is vital to the very existence of a committee.

At another, he mustered a few ill-chosen words on the ease with which communications, plain English notwithstanding, can break down within any group.

Loose didn't see that they were getting anywhere. But to his surprise, at 5:03 P.M. Miss Jacobus presented him with a sturdy seven-part skeleton:

1. An opening observation and complaint:

> all the sell
> has gone to hell

2. The importance of disagreement
within any committee; when men
in business together always agree,
all but one of them are unnecessary:

> *vive la différence!*

3. The importance of communications
within any organization:

> you can't be anti-semantic

4. An examination of an eternal verity:

> nothing requires constant
> reexamination so much as
> the obvious

5. How Fort Lauderdale solved problems
more like those confronting Memphis
than one might at first glance think:

> let's applauderdale
> **Fort Lauderdale!**

6. How Foote, Loose & Fancy was able
to assist in a civic project:

> a case history (with
> names fictionalized
> to protect parties
> involved)

7. As Cinderella discovered—
beauty often leads to bounty:

> proposed: 5000 more trees
> and 50 less billboards
> each year for Memphis!

Encouraged, Loose and Miss Jacobus set their
streams of consciousness to flowing, after a period
of which they painlessly produced the parts of
the speech, and proceeded then to accessorize
them from the closet we now open:

DRESS IT UP

The Madison Avenue Speech Book endorses 21 categories of podium-proved accessories. Even most Madison Avenue speeches, of course, would feel overdressed wearing examples of all of them. But any speech can gainfully employ a good many (especially since they often tend to cluster together in constellations, and sometimes even combine with one another as double or triple stars). Where helpful, we include illustrations from actual speeches. Some may seem rough-hewn. Yet all werc successful, and while our temptation was to improve those that could use it, for historical accuracy we have not.

FUNNY STORIES

Of course the best way to distract an audience is to make it laugh. Everybody knows funny stories do this. Everybody *doesn't* know funny stories also given an audience permission to laugh later on at whatever else in a speech is funny. Without being properly primed with funny stories, audiences have been known not to crack a smile during even very funny speeches. Any speech whose tenor permits should begin with two short funny stories, the second shorter and funnier than the first. A funny story does double duty if it makes an appropriate point. With a little ingenuity you can usually file an adequate point onto most funny stories. But a hilarious story that doesn't make a point is often better than an indifferently funny one that does. In any event, the odds are with the speaker: funny stories, even corn-fed ones, are more likely to evoke more laughter when told before a group than when privately related.

VISUAL AIDS

Accompany your remarks with interesting visual aids (never dreary charts or graphs) for your listeners to look at as they listen, and what they hear seems better than it is. A visual aid is also a superb camouflage—whenever an audience is looking at one it's not looking at you. The ultimate sophistication of the visual aid in the camouflage department is the slide or movie talk, which permits a speech to be delivered in darkness with speaker (and nervousness) invisible. The single most memorable element in many a successful speech has been a visual aid. Indeed many speeches, perhaps none more celebrated than Nathan Hale's farewell address, are remembered entirely because of one.

Annual Picnic Committee Chairman Dorothy Wessner unveiled a large color poster of the SS *Lorelei,* on which she proposed that this year's participants might sail to and from this year's site.

City Planner Ed Knowles displayed a large rendering which showed his plan for transforming downtown Secaucus into a verdant oasis.

Milliner Caesar added a visual fillip to his visual aid by showing some new hats on models dressed in gunnysacks, in order to focus attention on his hats.

Management Consultant Jonathan Loose dumped onto the stage a large paper bag of newspaper clippings which he declared were the results of a single season's promotional effort by the Fort Lauderdale Chamber of Commerce.

Fashion Expert Maggie Daly delivered most of a speech from behind a screen over which only her head could be seen, and where, as she talked, she was changing into clothes she would now and then briefly emerge to show.

AUDIO AIDS

The most helpful audio aids, any speaker in the act of speaking will agree, are an audience's applause and (when appropriate) its laughter. Often a way to create the climate for both is with sound effects, which at least never fail to sharpen a point.

Suburban Home Owner William Pemble kept tooting an old-fashioned automobile horn during his appeal to townsfolk to resist the rezoning of a residential neighborhood for business.

Lions Club Treasurer Jack Randall used bursts of wild cheers and applause (which he had taped from a live Metropolitan Opera broadcast) to punctuate proposals in his budget message to members.

Church Bazaar Chairman Louisa White repeatedly rang up imaginary sales on a borrowed cash register to lend venal immediacy to her plea for donations of goods.

Merchandising Executive Peter Greeman used the recorded sound of a jet plane taking off as a fanfare introducing the presentation of a new "jet age" line to his sales force.

DEMONSTRATIONS

Visual and audio aids become doubly effective when turned into demonstrations. Here the speaker uses props either to make a dramatic comparison or to make something happen—or both. The Madison Avenue adman uses demonstrations to make television commercials powerful—the white glove on the greasy scalp, the hair spray so clear you can't see it when it's sprayed on a mirror, the man flying into the driver's seat—and, because they're so absorbing, demonstrations are right up the Madison Avenue speaker's avenue too.

Amateur Chinese Chef Walter Neubau, with cleaver, chopping block and hotplate, demonstrated correct procedures for effecting Moo Goo Gai Pan.

Decorator Michael Greer, with large swatches of elegant fabrics, demonstrated the difference between what he alleged were good color schemes and bad.

Coiffeur Ernie Adler demonstrated do–it–yourself-able hairdos to make the thin face fuller and the full face thinner.

Art Dealer Michael St. Clair, in a defense of abstract art, demonstrated the subtle differences between an abstract he himself had painted in his basement the week before and a Jackson Pollock.

Conductor Leonard Bernstein—New York Philharmonic, prop—demonstrated the difference between early and final versions of Beethoven's 5th Symphony.

Bird Watcher Mary Beth Trautwein demonstrated the difference between the call of the nutting and that of the hatching female nuthatch.

Account Executive Lord G. Lord demonstrated the difference between automotive and lipstick advertising by showing slides of an automobile ad prepared as though it were a lipstick ad and a lipstick ad prepared as though it were an automobile ad.

quotes

Buttress your points, whether or not they need it, with apt quotations. Audiences oddly enough admire borrowers little less than authors of brilliant quotes, any luster of which rubs off generously on a talk. Entire successful speeches have been little more than conglomerates of other people's remarks. Adjusting a quote to make it apply can't hurt anything if the quote's obscure, can be amusing if it's famous. The Bible is a unique treasure-trove of quotes, not just because of its prestige, but because one place or another it says almost anything you hope it will. However, speakers intent on sugar-quoting their speeches, who can't find quotes that make the points they want them to, have also been known to make them up. These they sometimes attribute to G. K. Chesterton, since nobody's sure quite what all G. K. Chesterton said. Quoting a man also creates the illusion of familiarity with his entire body of work, presenting proof of education honored nearly everywhere. (Neglect to say, on the other hand, who said something, and many will indeed assume just you said it.)

LITERARY NUGGETS

Add tone to any talk by chipping some 24k nuggets from their original settings in literature—mythology, history, fiction or biography—and using them to illustrate what you're talking about. They have a way of making whatever parallel you're drawing seem not just vivid, but valid.

An anthropologist declared that giant corporations, in demanding uniformity from their executives, treat them as Procrustes treated his guests, either stretching them or cutting off their legs to make them fit the bed he had.

A railroad vice-president branded the fireman on an electric locomotive as less productive even than Penelope, who unraveled by night what she wove by day.

A nominee for public office observed that the incumbent was like the Red Queen in *Through the Looking Glass,* who had to run at top speed to stay in one place.

A commencement speaker feared too many young people today lacked a passion for financial independence and were like Shaw, who, as a young man, threw his mother rather than himself into the struggle for existence.

Homey Sayings

Homey sayings endear speakers to their audiences. The more high-busted a speaker or his station in life, the more endearing their effect. They are also mistaken for epigrams. Run down to the henhouse and gather an apron full. Or, since almost any simple thought can be turned into a grand homey saying merely by expressing it in 4-H Club terms, lay your own. Khrushchev's ancient Russian proverbs sound no less authentic for being, undoubtedly, written to fit. Rustic imagery is also good as Aunt Nell's elderberry turnovers for similes.

> "If you don't like the heat, stay
>   out of the kitchen."
>   —Harry Truman

> "It's the sheared sheep that grows new wool."
>   —Jonathan Loose

> "Her heart was as cold as a depot stove."
>   —*Ibid.*

local grace notes

If he is talking in a town, or to a group, other than his own, the Madison Avenue speaker never fails somehow to compliment the audience, and often also wisely takes care to mention an item or two of concern only to the town or group. Such local grace notes delight, and for some reason astonish, any audience. Revealing himself privy to purely parochial matters makes a speaker seem not just likeable, but somehow omniscient. Nobody ever seems able to imagine how he came by the information. Yet material for local grace notes is limitlessly available from any program chairman and local newspapers.

In her talk, "The Antelope Know," delivered to the Ashtabula Women's Civic Forward Club, Wyoming Naturalist Myrtle Markle briefly lamented the ruinous rain which occurred during the Club's tulip festival the past spring.

In his talk, "Our Warm Friend, the Sun," delivered to the science faculty of the Camden Public School

System, Princeton Physicist Dr. Joel Schumacher carried the local grace note device to its effective extreme by mentioning several members of the audience by name (pronouncing these names correctly), and saluting their particular individual contributions to science.

ATTACKS

Since a good defense is always a good offense, spring to an attack. An attack can singlehandedly provide the caffeine to assure a good night's sleepless audience. But naturally you can't get much traction attacking abstract bogeys, like Sloth. Or perennially attacked ones, like the departure of Christ from Christmas. Better you should attack a rarely attacked—or better still, an allegedly worthy—phenomenon of interest to your audience . . . and best of all one unlikely to retaliate.

Before an audience of fashion executives, another fashion executive attacked a citadel of learning. (". . . It's almost *tu*ition vs. *in*tuition: can we afford to put all those horn-rimmed method-trained young men from the Harvard School of Business —those early Jimmy Stewart types, eyes downcast, pawing the ground—into positions of authority in a business that's more madness than method? . . ." *et seq.*)

Before an audience of airline stewardesses, an airline safety expert attacked airline pilots.

("... I've even found them playing backgammon at the controls. ..." *et seq.*)

Before an audience of automotive admen, a non-automotive adwoman attacked the audience. ("... Too many advertising men are certain that the way to inject a feminine note into an ad—to hit women where they live—is to put an orchid corsage in a celluloid box on the back seat of the Buick. ..." *et seq.*)

SHOCKS

The Madison Avenue speaker cherishes shocks for their residual as well as their immediate effect, since good ones can leave everybody mentally—if not physically—murmuring on. There are three categories of shocks:

a. Shocks shocking because of who says them:

"The most dangerous word of all
in advertising is—*originality*."
> —Rosser Reeves
> (*famous for originality*
> *in advertising*)

b. Shocks shocking because of how they're said:

"Memphis is a (PAUSE) dead (PAUSE) city (PAUSE). Her buildings are overgrown with weeds, her markets lie empty of goods, her boulevards are untraveled, thick with shifting sand, and no river queens moor at her wharves. Yes, Memphis is a (PAUSE) dead (PAUSE) city (PAUSE). I have been describing Memphis, Egypt, not Tennessee, but it can happen here if we don't . . ." *et seq.*
> —Jonathan Loose

c. Shocks shocking no matter who says them
or how they're said:

"I am almost incapable of logical thought, but
I have developed techniques for keeping open the
telephone line to my unconscious, in case that
disorderly repository has anything to tell me. I
hear a great deal of music. I am on friendly terms
with John Barleycorn. I take long hot baths. I
spend an hour at stool every day."
—David Ogilvy

VITALIZED STATISTICS

Statistics, which in numerical form always stultify, can enliven a speech when translated into word pictures that the audience can look and wonder at. The more picturesque they are, the less their accuracy seems to be questioned.

"Do you have any idea how large the national debt really *is*? Why, enough dollar bills to carpet the entire state of Tennessee wall-to-wall couldn't pay it off."
                                        —Jonathan Loose

doctoRẏed cliches

Because they are so familiar, clichés plod past not even heard, let alone seen, in the mind of the audience. Like the tickings of clocks or mattresses, they just don't register—leaving little vacuums, or at best threadbare patches, damaging to a speech. Let your opportunities not be golden, your flashes not blinding, your junior executives not bright-eyed and bushy-tailed, your queens not every inch them. Yet by giving their spinelessness a wrench, you can snap clichés—and your listeners—smartly to attention.

> *(a representative of a tourist board, glamorizing an island:)*
>
> "Come to Jamaica—it's no place like home."

> *(a union official, itemizing complaints against the company:)*
>
> "As for the cafeteria, it offers a cuisine second to any."

*(a medical student, tracing the
history of a vaccine:)*

> "But here was a cure
> for which there was
> no known disease."

*(a prize-winning gardener, minimizing
the importance of a green thumb:)*

> "Really all you do is
> weed and reap."

*(a morticians' association president,
describing to members the bungling
of a sale of a costly casket:)*

> ". . . thereby, at the
> last moment, snatching
> defeat from the jaws of
> victory."

PUNS

You always make hay when the pun shines. But the gift of being able to tell bright from frightful punwise is distributed more liberally among audiences than speakers. The wise speaker never confuses the joy of discovering a pun with the wisdom of using it. In fact, he often tests his puns on others, and lets their judgment, not his, decide whether to include or omit them. Puns are especially adept at fitting clichés for human consumption, and barbing them to stick in the mind.

(a women's college provost, asserting the equality of women to men in business:)

"A miss is as good as a male."

(a home-appliance manufacturer, reminding his salesmen that bigger sales mean bigger commissions:)

"The wife you save may be your own."

*(a carpet company's home economist,
ticking off the virtues of carpet:)*

"Carpet covers a multitude of dins."

*(a department store executive, preaching
the gospel of thrift:)*

"Don't be an incomepoop."

*(a teacher, deploring polysyllabic
English of Latin root:)*

"Fill sentences, instead, with
Anglo-Saxon pith and vinegar."

COINED LABELS

Coining a new label for anything automatically gives you something fresh, different and interesting to talk about. Coined labels are such shining stars for hitching wagons to that advertising has always been full of them: B.O., Tired Blood, Pink Toothbrush, Dirt Backwash.

They not only can describe the existing . . .

> "An *iron curtain* has descended across the continent."
> —Winston Churchill

but make the non-existing exist . . .

> "But the *New Frontier* of which I speak is not a set of promises— it is a set of challenges."
> —John F. Kennedy

ENCAPSULATED SUMMINGS UP

Whenever a speaker encapsulates a whole kettle of fish in a kindergarten-simple summing up he can't help but seem in command of his material and himself. Actually, these minor miracles of miniaturization are usually little more than gross oversimplifications, which the neatness of their package conceals.

Instead of saying, "Success in the cosmetic business today depends upon your merchandise, and upon what your advertising can legitimately claim your merchandise will do, and also, of course, upon making money," a speaker said:

> "Mind your three p's of cosmetics:
> product, promise, profit."

Instead of saying, "Despite the fact that we're in a terrible depression, with millions out of work and more millions hungry, when you come right down to it we really haven't got so much as we think we have to be frightened of," a speaker said:

> "The only thing we have
> to fear is fear itself."

clarion calls to arms

A speaker who is (or wishes to be mistaken for someone who is) secure in the saddle may include a clarion call to arms, close cousin of the encapsulated summing up. But besides encapsulating, proper ones ennoble disagreeable chores. And make everybody want to run get their girdle on.

Instead of saying, "In the conduct of your businesses the choice must often arise between a decision which will benefit only you, and one which will benefit your community as well," a speaker said:

> "MEMPHIS begins with the letters M-E.
> Let not it *end* there."

Instead of saying, "The job ahead of us isn't easy; a lot of people are going to get killed, and every one of us will have to pitch in, often in the face of great personal sorrow," a speaker said:

> "I have nothing to offer but
> blood, toil, tears and sweat."

$\mathscr{FABLES}$

Audiences, like children, like fables. Set a scene in the forest, stock it with furred or feathered friends, and tell a tale. Don't worry if the plot merely points up a platitude. Fables are like animal crackers: shape enhances content. People never fail to accept a fable's denouement as wisdom, its moral as wit.

the fable of the
weasel and the squirrel

Once upon a time, on Madison Lane, there were two advertising agencies, one run by a squirrel, the other by a weasel.

One day the squirrel's account executives could be seen pitching a tent over the sleeping form of their biggest client, a warthog.

When the weasel saw the squirrel himself scampering along the lane, he ran out to inquire the purpose of the tent.

"Our research told us it was going to rain," the squirrel explained proudly as, sure enough, thunder crashed and a downpour began.

The weasel humphed and replied: "Our research told us the same thing. But we hit upon the idea of waking our clients and telling them to go in out of the rain."

"A little obvious, don't you think?" murmured the squirrel, wishing he'd thought of that.

"Obvious, shmobvious," said the weasel, his smug expression lit by lightning as it struck a nearby mushroom, "it works."

The two executives stood discussing business for some time.

"Say," said the squirrel finally, "not to change the subject or anything, but I'm getting positively soaked."

"Mercy!" cried the weasel, streaking for cover, "me too!"

moral: nothing requires constant reexamination so much as the obvious

—Jonathan Loose

DOGGEREL

A bit of original doggerel permits a display of what will be interpreted as virtuosity. The doggerel needn't scan. But it must amuse. Amusing rhymes—clever, topical, irreverent, unlikely or contrived—create the illusion of amusing lines, and require no more than a little patience to achieve. (Beware of greeting-card rhymes, like June/moon and love/dove; they make an audience Nash its teeth unless they happen to make amusing sense.)

> You've seen how an ad which promises
> a woman the moon delights her
>
> And how advertising as a profession
> is actually missionary work after
> the heart of Albert Schweitzer.
>
> But you can't promise a girl a trip
> to the moon and then let her down in
> Levittown, Pennsylvania:
>
> If your ads make a fool of her she may
> just pick up a twenty-seven dollar and
> fifty cent jar of your product and brainia.

If you write cosmetic advertising you
have to resist the temptation to lie,
or indulge in magician's sleight-of-hand
or hat tricks . . .

Particularly if your office, like mine,
looks down on the roof of St. Patrick's.

Fantastic product claims can be made
today only if the lab comes up with a
bona fide miracle . . .

You can't expect an advertising agency
to make a silk purse from a sow's ear—
or a square product spherical.

For ads are written by fools like David
Ogilvy and me . . .

And even David can't make a tree.

Although I suspect that Rosser Reeves

Just might be able to make the leaves.
—Kay Daly

SONGS

It's to leaven the lump of the sermon that songs are sung in church. Songs can breathe life into speeches, too. The song should be a parody of one with familiar words and music. The parody needn't be clever, for parodies are presumed clever. Don't worry if you can't carry a tune. Songs sung by tone-deaf speakers have been applauded louder than many sung by Martha Wright. But musical accompaniment is essential. If you're diffident about soloing, have the lyrics mimeographed and distributed to the audience so it can sing along.

In a speech to the St. Louis Shoe Manufacturers Association, Bernice Fitz-Gibbon, accompanied on the violin, toasted the decline of the bosom as a fashion accessory with:

June ain't bustin' out all over
Her bosom's been flattened by Dior
With her bust no longer busty
With her curves no longer lusty
All the menfolk's eyes are straying to the floor.

How can Junie keep her sex appeal
With bosoms no longer in the news?
It's so easy if she's clever
She'll be sexier than ever
If she concentrates on buying sexy shoes.

It's sexy shoes
Shoes, shoes, shoes
June needs sexy shoes, shoes, shoes!

STUNTS

Defined, a stunt is any byplay or business you arrange to occur that otherwise normally wouldn't during a speech. That gives one's imagination free rein. But choosing a stunt to enliven a speech requires the care of choosing a carpet in the casbah. Even the best stunts are risky; the only sure way to try the mettle of one is, alas, to try it. We mention them only because when successful they're usually so *very* successful for Madison Avenue purposes; we might more wisely omit them because when unsuccessful they're usually so disastrous. Stunts sometimes require speakers to be made bits of fools of, which, if dignity of speech and speaker permit, audiences adore. The best stunts are probably ones which can't positively be identified as such. Except at conventions, avoid baldly slapstick stunts—shooting off a pistol to get attention, having workmen come in to pound a few nails, arranging for the collapse of the head table, etc., while you're on.

Stunts are highly personalized affairs, but:

A politician had "hecklers" in the audience interrupt his speech occasionally with rude remarks which he handled with exquisite grace and courtesy.

A toastmaster had someone enter and leave the room several times through a door which, when opened, admitted the sound of a rehearsal of *Rigoletto*.

A falconist, talking with cunningly trained falcon strapped to wrist, had the bird "escape" and flap about the hall.

A shop steward, desiring his talk to appear more fiery than it was, had two members of the audience engage in a physical scuffle over—and during—his remarks, which terminated in their ejection from the room.

An honored guest, concerned about the bone-brevity of his speech, had the people sitting at the head table apparently drop off, one by one, to sleep, giving him an excuse to "cut short" his talk.

Question **&**
Answer periods

The Madison Avenue speaker usually avoids a question & answer period at the end of his speech, lest it reveal how little of what he's been talking about he actually knows. However, speakers have had notable success—demonstrating tip-of-the-tongue erudition and trigger wit—with question & answer periods for which they prepare the questions (together with a cut-off device to cut the questioning off). These they distribute confidentially in advance among trusties in the audience who are, of course, the only questioners they recognize. They also, you may be sure, prepare the answers, and my how brilliant *they* can be.

cutting
remarks

Unless you're superhuman, each part of your speech has turned out longer than it should be. *Good.* A speech is like a statue, much of the merit of which depends upon what's cut away. Unlike a statue, the more it's cut, the better it gets. Take particular care to:

cut anything that doesn't clearly state meaning, illustrate it, or amuse

cut syntactical filigree—by far the best sentence
is the simple declarative

cut transitions, and step as directly
as possible from part to part

cut generalizations and abstractions:
efficacious measures and foremost considerations

cut pomposities: don't let birds form
annual autumnal caravans to the southlands

cut personifications: Grim Reapers
and Dames Fortune

cut forced alliterations: no lumbering
leviathans

cut time-tattered similes:
strong as an ox, rich as Croesus

cut parasitic facts: unless it contributes, don't
reveal that George Washington had a sister Betty

cut the cornily cute or darling, like references to
babies as members of the carriage trade

cut passages which express thoughts in "other
words" unless these words are better—then cut
the original words and just use the other words

cut adjectives along for the ride, like the ones in
trained technicians and creative imagination

cut euphemisms: if you can't say somebody
died instead of passed away, forget it

cut Illinois off Chicago, France off Paris

cut till you can't see how you can cut any more,
and then . . .

CUT
SOME
MORE

N.B.: Because they are little autonomies of their own, free of connective tendon, entire parts of a Madison Avenue speech can also often be quickly and cleanly cut should need arise.

EVEN HAMLET
HAD A GHOST

Some people can't be bothered writing their speeches. Others not only find words more tools than toys, but crude ones at that. These speakers often carry the advice to enlist all possible help from others to the length of having someone write their entire speeches for them. It is easiest to get someone to perform this service if he already works for you. But money paid—or being married, related or close friend—to anyone familiar with the Madison Avenue technique (and able to write a speech) helps. The Madison Avenue speaker never lets pride or jealousy of authorship deter him from calling upon a ghost; he knows that the act of delivering a speech convinces any speaker he really wrote it all himself. Even if rehearsal weren't necessary for other reasons, it would be essential for a ghostwritten speech, to be sure he could articulate everything in it. (As, indeed, it also would be for one he wrote himself.)

get a hearing aid

The ear is a less efficient tool than the eye. Writing written to be heard should be simple, and comprehensible (except for any technical matter, and better it too) to an unprecocious twelve-year-old child. So why not test your speech on an unprecocious twelve-year-old child? Muddiness of sense and syntax not apparent to you immediately shows up as muddy to it. Then rewrite and retest till the all-clear signal sounds. (Or, at least, read your speech to disinterested persons and fix it if they remain disinterested.) With text cut and clear, rehearse. Rehearsal keeps a written speech, which naturally must either be read or memorized, from sounding wooden, and really diligent rehearsal can positively silverplate the tongue. Tape-recording a rehearsal to hear for himself how others will hear him never fails to be helpful to a speaker, whether it results, as usual, in improvement or, as occasional, in the peremptory decision to cancel the talk. The more rehearsed, the less rehearsed any speech sounds.

"I am the most spontaneous speaker in the world because every word, every gesture and every retort has been carefully rehearsed."

—George Bernard Shaw

DELIVERY CHARGES

On rising to talk, omit the Birdseye Frozen Smile. Then instead of trying to be something else, be what you've had a lifetime of practice being: yourself. Don't try to make your speaking voice different from your unspeaking voice. Preserve any vocal eccentricity—accent, twang, stridency, etc.—that contributes color. Loudness is often accepted as conviction. Let your voice emphasize particular points. But stress everything and of course you stress nothing. Vary volume. Surround loudnesses with softnesses. A well-placed whisper can drown out surrounding shouts. Within reason, pause = poise, provided you don't clutter your pauses up with *ers* and *uhs*. Indeed, moments in a speech filled with silence can say more, moment for moment, than those filled with words. Don't let rigor mortis set in. Plan, via a little choreography, to be your own visual aid. Move around a bit, gesture, look here and there, lean on the lectern, draw yourself back up to full height, as you feel like it. While you never want to seem to be fighting off a host of hornets, it's better to be over-animated than under-.

Pragmatic Notes

A Madison Avenue speech is surely the easiest and best of all possible speeches to prepare and to give. But still easier, and often still better, than giving one is not giving one. If you haven't gotten out of your speech in time not to write it, maybe you can in time not to give it. The true Madison Avenue speaker speaks voluntarily for only three reasons:

a. he's being paid

b. he's appearing before a group whose opinion can help sustain or better his lot

c. he's urging the audience to commit some Act it would otherwise not, the benefit from which somehow accrues to him

He knows that falling for flattery gets him nowhere, and never lets the flattery implicit or explicit in an invitation to speak bewitch him into accepting it. He never quickly descends to bait which he realizes has probably already been spurned; most prospective speakers are approached as a second or third—or last—resort.

Promises that he'll be sharing the podium with a celebrity of the stature of Edward Stone & up are not uncommon but beguile him not, for such celebrities rarely show.

He's aware that declining to speak for an "honorarium"—that genteelism for an all but non-fee—is what often separates the real pros from the pose pros.

He won't say he'll talk six months from now believing six months from now won't come. He knows it will. And faster than it would have.

Once he's decided to make his speech he doesn't moon evasively about like somebody who's going to get married and doesn't want to. He gets a wiggle on.

If he's frightened at the prospect of his talk, he tries to think of his fear as a *friend* . . . a friend that will make him so much better than he would have been that he may even learn to love his panic. He tries *not* to think of the most common disadvantage of Madison Avenue speaking—that he'll talk so well he'll be badgered to talk again.

He doesn't worry if his speech has more glitter than gold: it's safer to delight than to edify. Ideas disturb. So does making people think; audiences characteristically have their do-not-disturb signs hanging on their mental doorknobs and wish to remain fast asleep within.

Yet he tries not to be full of pale permission for everything. On the contrary, he often goes out of his way to appear frankly biased. For any audience is more interested by a biased viewpoint it doesn't agree with than an unbiased one it does.

He doesn't let personal encounters with great names drop too trippingly from his tongue. Unless he acts a little (yet not too) impressed by the chat he says he had with pope, prime minister or president, nobody will think he had it—or like him if they think he had.

When talking about a great or famous name, he often drops in a pertinent juicy little-known "human interest" morsel about same. Knowledge of backstairs detail, besides being irresistibly interesting, puts a speaker on something of a footing with the person described and can completely remove the onus of name-dropping from name-dropping . . . although often, to be sure, a more accurate label for this material is gossip.

An easy way to help make any speech seem fresh as damp ink on the morning newspaper is, at the last minute, to pop in a highly topical item that occurred only that very day or the day before.

An easy way synthetically to inject interest into a speech is to emulate the television comedians who synthetically inject humor into their programs simply by "harking back" to material established earlier, thereby developing and playing upon a "situation."

He doesn't antagonize his audience by making it participate in his speech except to listen, laugh, applaud and perhaps sing, the only things it will willingly do. He doesn't suggest that the people say good morning or good evening to him, as one leading speech authority recommends, nor raise their hands, nor pass anything around, nor introduce themselves to their neighbors, nor march around the breakfast table, nor stand or move for any purpose except to flee in case of fire.

He recognizes the most universally despised form of participation as requiring an audience to dig into its pockets then and there for a cause.

He may, however, ask people on the periphery of a large audience whether they're having difficulty hearing him (although this may have been their hope in sitting there).

If he is speaking as a member of a firm, he discourages a "company table," sparing himself the further ordeal of talking before a concentrated nest of well-wishing daily associates . . . which he often accurately suspects wishes him not so well as it pretends. Instead, he tries to scatter such people through the hall where they can, if they're a-mind, laugh and applaud louder and oftener than they delicately could as part of a patently partisan group.

It is not entirely unknown for a Madison Avenue speaker deliberately to recruit a claque to whip up laughter and applause at prearranged points in a speech.

If he reads his speech, he does so from 3 × 5 cards on which his text has been typed. Because the cards are so small, they make a speech seem shorter than it would seem if read from full-size sheets. He permits there to be no pitcher or glass or other visible reserve of fresh water to convey the impression that he's prepared for a siege.

When addressing luncheons a
often assures at least gastrointes
eating elsewhere, and letting the c
croquette, neath its polished pink sa

He keeps an eye on his props, if a
waiter remove them with the dishes.

He realizes that martinis sharpen his
only if they're in his audience and not i
and won't chance even the tiniest Scotcl
waterloo.

It may seem egotistical, but he himself wri
the introductory remarks for the person wi
will introduce him. Thus he assures his bein
bathed from the beginning in the light he
wishes, with no neon-powered exaggerations or
embarrassing inaccuracies . . . or accuracies.
Such an introduction should certainly contain
any personal plugs—for the book he has written, the product he makes, the skill he has to
sell—that he wishes not to be so crass as to
plug himself.

He is careful to repeat crucial phrases or
sentences that he wishes to italicize, or that
might be hard for the ear to catch.

He puts anything he wants people to do as
the result of his talk at the very end where—

pleased at having been diverted by a Madison Avenue, instead of bored by a conventional, speech—the audience is most receptive . . . not to mention most likely to remember what it is.

He never soars into metaphor and exhorts the folks to scrape the barnacles from our ship of state or anything that, even willing to do, they wouldn't know how.

In the relatively unlikely event that he is asked to prepare copies of his speech for the press, he may legitimately include in the press copies any remarks he wishes to publicize but doesn't care to say in person. Conversely, he may delete any he doesn't care to publicize but wishes to say.

However, he avoids submitting the text of his speech to the program people in advance. He may want to change it. Worse, they may.

When he begins, he *begins*. He ignores the circumstances which brought his appearance about ("Last August when I ran into Chairman Gillies in the lobby of the Greenbrier, little did I suspect . . ."). He doesn't apologize for anything (". . . that here I'd be in the role of amateur presuming to address the experts").

He avoids self-deprecation or overmodesty of any kind, if for no other reason than that it emblazons the scarlet letter A—for Amateur— on his breast.

He doesn't announce, warn, promise or threaten that he's going to end.

HE

ENDS

APPENDIX A

annotated verbatim text of a typical Madison Avenue speech

The fourth, and final, sensible reason to give a speech is that you're somehow compelled to.

Such was the case with Bennett Anderson, who was unable to avoid giving one before a dinner meeting of the League of Women Voters in the Sioux Room of the Last Scout Motor Lodge.

Anderson, a local architect, was head of the Building Subcommittee of the Citizens' Advisory Committee for the Tykestown Public Schools. As such, he had served for three years without having to make a public utterance.

Speeches were normally the province of the chairman of the parent committee, Rutherford B. Highs, who relished them, and who had, in fact, been originally scheduled to deliver this one: another plea for another school-bond issue.

But a week before the speech Highs slipped a disk and went, indefinitely, into traction. Other senior committee members were equally unavailable to appear. Mr. Marshall was camping near Loon Lake. Mr. Kildaire was in the throes of the thesis for his doctorate. Mrs. Hill was inextricably entangled in the Hospital Benefit Ball. It fell inexorably to Anderson, who dreaded public speaking, to talk.

His Madison Avenue speech, relatively modest effort though it was, earned gratifying, if not unbridled, applause. And, besides, it successfully concealed the fact that he couldn't have been more limp with fear, as he rose to speak, than had he been boned by the *maître d'hôtel*.

Let us reproduce it with no ado further than the caution that the text of any speech without prior fame to recommend it can look far less prepossessing than it sounds; words meant to be heard often seem as banal, when merely seen, as words meant to be sung, when merely read aloud.

(The distinguished president of the League, Mrs. Reginald Phipps-Williams, breathtakingly corseted, and with manner no less hyphenated than her name, gets things off to an auspicious start:)

Our principal speaker tonight is Mr. Bennet Anderson, Chairman of the Building Subcommittee of the Citizens' Committee for the Public Schools. Mr. Anderson is Tykestown's most distinguished architect. He is responsible for many of our loveliest homes, as well as our fabulous Frogg Hollow Country Club. As an architect, he is ideally qualified to chair the Building Subcommittee, which must naturally work closely with the school architects . . . with whom Mr. Anderson, of course, has no professional connection. Mr. Anderson.

introduction

personal plug

bathing in appropriate light

Thank you. My wife went to Sacred Heart Academy. She was on the debating team. One Saturday the boys' debating team from Mackenzie High came to debate. The boys were *for* capital punishment, the girls *agin*

he begins

funny story #1
(remember, people
are more easily
collectively than
individually amused)

it. The girls lost the debate, but that's not the point. After the debate my wife took it upon herself to take the boys on an impromptu tour of the school. They went through all the deserted classrooms and study halls and laboratories and finally through the vast empty library, stacks and all. Next day my wife was called to the Mother Superior's office. This virtuous lady had heard of the guided—or misguided—tour. She fixed a steely glance on Kathleen and said, "If you wake up some morning the victim of a tragedy you'll have only yourself to blame."

brief gratuitous
milking of
funny story #1

You ladies will forgive me if I don't take you on a tour of the motor lodge at the end of my speech.

PART I
(two new
schools needed)

funny story #2

Old John and Mary were in the twilight of their lives. They had been married 52 years. One evening as they sat together on the porch glider, John took Mary's hand tenderly. "Mary," he said, "we might as well face it. One of us has to go first." "Yes," said Mary sadly, "and when that happens I'm going to live in California."

88

You see, we never think it can happen to us. But it *has* happened to us, right here in Tykestown. We have outgrown our schools so fast that the staggered sessions and double sessions we thought would never come are now here. Our kids are cabin'd, cribb'd, confined. We need two new schools. We need a new high school. We need a new elementary school. And we can have them, open for business, in just three short years. Why, you may ask, must we build both schools at once? Wouldn't it be wiser—and certainly less of a financial burden—to build them one at a time?

no apologies or self-deprecation

> Aren't we making it pretty tough
> With taxes already so high?
> Isn't *one* new albatross enough?
> Without *two* new albatri?

doggerel

The answer is no, no, three times no. No *first* because we simply have to have both schools to eliminate staggered and double sessions in Tykestown. No *second* because schools built sooner will cost less than schools built later and, besides, we can get a "package price" for construction of both schools at a discount. And no *third* because new state aid is now available, and *both* schools will increase taxes less than a *sin-*

gle new school has in the past. Building *both* schools *now* is essential to providing the best feasible education with the best feasible economy. In fact, Tykestown's whole school problem is really a simple one of readin' and writin' and *thrift*-metic. Let's make that the title of this talk: readin' and writin' and *thrift*-metic.

encapsulated summing up / pun / repetition

PART II (choosing sites)

Ask any suburban mother to state her role in life in a sentence and she could answer: "To deliver children—obstetrically once, and by car forever after." We chose the proposed sites for our two new schools with this lament in mind. These sites are indicated in red on this map of the township. Notice that both are *within walking distance* of the major population centers of Tykestown. School-bus mileage will also be kept to a minimum by these sites. Of course, more than mere location is important in choosing a school site. Our proposed sites offer other crucial advantages as well. Contours of the land on both sites will require a minimum of grading for school and recreational construction. There's good existing drainage. No extensive new water or sewer lines need be laid. Prices of the sites —$2000 and $2320 an acre—are fair. The

quote (from Peter De Vries, whom Anderson elected not to identify)

visual aid

simple declarative sentences

90

state recommends 48 acres for a senior high school of the size we propose. Our high school site exceeds this by four acres. The elementary school site hits the state recommendation of 12 acres on the button. In addition, the high school site, you notice, is adjacent to the new Monatowompic Park area just ceded to the township by the county, where extensive recreational facilities will be available to students. Truly, these are sites for sore eyes.

doctored cliché / pun

Rumors of extravagance in the planning of our high school have been circulating in the community. Until recently it seemed that these rumors were being spread—and being believed—by an ineffectual group organized only by its opposition, for one reason or another, to the new high school. Until recently, opposition to the high school has been a matter of the bland leading the bland. But lately the rumors and the gossip have been stepped up and intensified. Lately they have been getting pretty good kill per gallon. For there has lately emerged in the community the articulate spokesman against the high school—the spokesman whom I call the *Mortimer Snide*. I call these people Mortimer Snides because they

PART III (opposition to schools) no transitions

doctored cliché / pun

coined label

91

only *seem* to be articulate. Actually they are dummies on the laps of anonymous ventriloquists who oppose the school. Their arguments are mined with misinformation. The Mortimer Snides have particularly seized upon the proposed cost of $20 per square foot for the high school. They invariably compare this figure to the $14.59 per square foot which the new Milltown high school cost Milltown, less than 100 miles to the east. How, they ask, can a geographical difference of 100 miles increase the cost per square foot almost 50 percent? Surely, they say, here is evidence of extravagance to justify at least postponement of the school. The Mortimer Snides do not tell you the rest of the facts. The rest of the facts are these:

1. The town of Milltown, rather than the school district, buys and owns school property. Hence the cost of the property is not included in the cost of the school.

2. The Milltown school turns out to be a *junior* high school, less expensive to equip than the school we need, a *senior* high school.

3. In Milltown, the wage scale for skilled

construction labor is a full dollar per hour less than in Tykestown.

For these and other reasons, our price of $20 per square foot in Tykestown is actually *better* than the $14.59 price in Milltown.

In front of mixed audiences, most speakers close their eyes—and mouths—to another important source of opposition to new public school construction: the Catholics. (mild) *shock* Many Catholics feel they have enough of a burden supporting their own schools without also supporting public schools which their children do not attend. These Catholics are wrong. It is the rightful burden of all of us to support the public schools regardless of where we elect to send our children, and regardless, in fact, of whether we even *have* any children. I am a Catholic. My wife is a Catholic. One of our daughters is in a Catholic junior college and was educated entirely in Catholic schools. Nevertheless I am so convinced that a fine *public* school system is the very foundation of a healthy community that I have served for several years now as chairman of the Building Subcommittee.

the fable of the mother goose and the childless gander

fable

Once upon a time there was a mother goose and a gander who was childless.

The mother goose was a member of the Citizens' Committee for the Public Schools. One day she approached the childless gander to urge him to vote yes for the new school-bond issue.

harking back

"Why should I vote yes and raise my taxes when I have no child to educate?" demanded the gander. "Wouldn't that be hanging an albatross around my own neck?"

"Indeed not," said the mother goose. "The new school is for the good of us all. But even if it weren't," she continued, "haven't you heard the saying, 'What's an albatross for the goose is an albatross for the gander'?"

"That settles it," said the gander, who went directly off and voted yes.

moral: nothing is so simple in real life as it is in a fable

It took two years of study to evolve the plan for the new high school. The plan is the result of the complete cooperation of the Citizens' Committee, the School Faculty, the School Administrators, and the architects, Burr & Hamilton. We owe a major debt to the League of Women Voters for its foresight in providing the funds for a preliminary design study three years ago, on which our further study was based. Several members of the League have worked hard on the various committees since, among them Miss Anastasia Schwartz, Mrs. Meriwether Sloan, and Mrs. Inigo Jones. Before we inspect the floor plan of the school, may we have the slide of the exterior rendering prepared by the architects.

(The houselights dim and a slide of the Parthenon, with Anderson and his wife in front of it waving, flashes on the screen. Laughter.)

I'm sorry. May we have the *school* slide, please.

(The Parthenon is replaced by the Tower of London, Mr. and Mrs. Anderson in front, waving. Laughter.)

May I have the *school* slide *please*. Thank

PART IV
(the high school)

pinpointed subjects

audience compliment

local grace note

stunt

95

you. Now, notice what a handsome school the architects propose. Burr & Hamilton have achieved their economy and efficiency with, clearly, no sacrifice of architectural beauty. Now the slide of the floorplan, please. The shape of the building is an open quadrangle. The interior court provides natural light and air for the interior. The quadrangle plan cuts corridor length and area. The classroom wing on the west is two stories. This permits standard classrooms and science rooms to be centralized for good administration. Special classrooms, labs, and the library, cafeteria, auditorium, gymnasium and other necessities which resist multistory arrangement, are arranged in single-story sequence on the north, east and south sides of the building. Yet all are convenient to the classroom wing. Noisy places, like the shops and music rooms, are soundproofed by their location. We've made provision for a new two-story 20-classroom wing to be built at right angles to the original classroom wing to increase capacity to 1600 pupils when necessary. Waste space has been virtually eliminated. Note the absence of a swimming pool—a costly and unproductive indulgence. Our proposed design has no frills.

Planning our elementary school was made easier because it will be a carbon copy—almost—of our enormously successful Tykestown Dells school built three years ago—Burr & Hamilton, architects. Tykestown Dells has in fact become a model for new elementary schools all over the state. Last October I couldn't believe my ears when I answered the phone and it was Governor Slathers himself on the line. He wanted to see Tykestown Dells for himself, and drove down from the capital next week to do so. He was astonished by the combination of beauty, utility and economy of Tykestown Dells. Astonishing our Governor with economy is no easy affair. The Governor is a very frugal man. At one point I wanted to write down a comment he made, but I had no paper handy. The Governor handed me an envelope which he said he was carrying as scrap paper. I wrote down what I wanted to and was about to put the whole envelope in my pocket. But the Governor took the envelope, tore off the part I had written on, which he gave me, and then put the rest of the envelope back in his own pocket for future use. "You never miss the milk till the cow runs dry," he said. But our new elementary school will

PART V
(the elementary school)

name-drop

"human interest" morsel

quote / homey saying

97

quote

differ from Tykestown Dells in several slight particulars. In the words of Frank Lloyd Wright, "To know a building, one must live in it." We have lived in it, and the changes—we trust the improvements— are these: We've switched the auditorium and the cafeteria around. Instead of four kindergarten rooms, we'll have two, leaving two rooms for physically and mentally handicapped children. By using existing grades we can use the economical "scissors stair," with a climb of only one-half flight up or down from the main corridor to the upper- or lower-story classrooms . . . and no waste space for a central stairwell. We're recommending toilets for outside use. And we have included outside doors to each classroom on the lower level.

PART VI
(cost)

topical item

Figures are boring. We won't dwell on them. The whole works that we are proposing comes to 4½ million dollars, give or take a dollar. Just yesterday Mayor Broome broke ground for our new municipal sports arena, which will cost over 5 million. If we can afford 5 million for sports, I guess we can afford 4½ million for schools. Our proposals will increase taxes just $5.60 for each $1000 of assessed valuation. $3.70 will go for the high school. $1.60 will go for the elementary school. This adds up to $5.30 or 30 cents *less* than $5.60. What are we going to do with that 30 cents? Well, we propose to buy, and at bargain prices, two additional sites for still another high school and still another elementary school which will eventually become necessary as Tykestown grows. 30 little cents. An amount so small it's hardly worth keeping.

some longer, some shorter, but parts average their budgeted three minutes

> (*Anderson tosses a handful of 30 pennies over his shoulder to clatter down on the platform.*)

vitalized statistic / video aid / audio aid / demonstration

When the Planet Uranus was discovered, Dr. Watson mentioned the discovery to Sherlock Holmes, and Holmes was annoyed. Sherlock Holmes said he had no room in his head for useless information, and would now have to go to the trouble of *forgetting* about the Planet Uranus. I know that the minds of you busy ladies are also full. Ladies of the League of Women Voters, you don't have to remember this speech. All I ask you to remember is just one little word, and that word is YES. All you have to remember is to vote "YES" for the new school-bond issue on referendum day, June 19. *A word to the wives is sufficient, and that word is* YES.

PART VII (vote yes)

literary nugget

clarion call to arms / doctored cliché / pun / repetition

May I introduce, to those few of you who've never heard her, Miss Grace Everglades, soprano soloist at Locust Lutheran Church. Grace will sing for us "The Song of the Vagabonds," from *The Vagabond King* by Rudolf Friml—first the way it was written, in order to refresh your memory, and then with a new set of lyrics. Each of you has a copy of the new lyrics at your place —please join in. Miss Everglades is accompanied on the Hammond by Mr. E. Third Power, organist at Locust Lutheran.

(Grace Everglades, singing:)

Sons of toil and danger
Will you serve a stranger
And bow down to Burgundy?

Sons of shame and sorrow
Will you cheer tomorrow
For the crown of Burgundy?

Onward, onward, swords against the foe!
Forward, forward the lily banners go!

Sons of France around us
Break the chain that bound us
And to hell with Burgundy!

(Grace Everglades and audience, singing:)

Better education
For a better nation . . .
We'll vote YES on June 19!

song
(no other audience participation suggested)

We have learned our lesson!
Kill the double session!
We'll vote YES on June 19!

Tykestown needs an elementary school!
And a high school (without a swimming
    pool)!

We are of a feather!
We will flock together
To vote YES on June 19!

Thank you, Grace. Remember, a word to
the wives is sufficient, and that word is YES.
Vote YES for the new school bond issue on
referendum day, June 19.

*what people are to
do placed at end
of talk /
repetition /
unheralded ending*

Q. Mr. Anderson, before you leave may I
    ask you if it isn't true that *actual* costs
    per square foot always exceed *estimated*
    costs per square foot?

*question
& answer period*

101

A. This is not true. The last school we built—Tykestown Dells—was estimated at $19.36 per square foot and actually cost, as completed, $14.21 per square foot. That's $5.15 per square foot *less* than the estimate.

Q. If the bond issue goes through, how much will our taxes be increased per pupil?

tip-of-the-tongue erudition

A. The two new schools will handle a total of 2055 pupils. If your present assessed property valuation is $5000—which is average—your proposed increase will be $28 a year, or little more than *one penny per pupil per year.*

Q. Perhaps double sessions aren't so bad as they're cracked up to be. I've heard the argument that since we've had double sessions, the Regents averages of our students have, in fact, gone up. Do you have an explanation?

A. If I may say so, this is an argument of a quicksliver mind. In Stockholm, prison officials decided to prove the curse of drink by staging a football match between the jail's chronic alcoholics and its other inmates. The alcoholics won! But does this prove the *merit* of drink? *No.* Our Regents averages have indeed gone up. But does this prove the *merit* of the double session? *No.* *trigger wit*

Q. You speak of a high school without frills. Maybe we can do without a swimming pool. But what is the dividing line today between the frill and the dress? I just read that a high school in Detroit has installed a fully equipped letterpress printing plant. Shouldn't we perhaps be considering specialized equipment too, even if it does increase the budget?

A. The Building Subcommittee feels that being able to boast of a fully equipped letterpress printing establishment is not only an extravagance, but a dubious distinction, like being a midget's midget. The function of a high school is to provide a good secondary education, and

103

not advanced technical training which is the province of the trade school or university. We propose no printing press. No planetarium. No astronomical observatory. No aviary. No electronics research center. No garage. No cyclotron. No surgery. No experimental farm. No aquarium. No foundry. No snail garden. No elegantly appointed atelier with north light for the budding artists of Tykestown who, if they're going to bud will bud anyway, without a lot of foolish Go, Van, Gogh.

cut-off device And, speaking of go, I'm sorry that *I've* got to go. I've just time to get to the station to catch the Water Level Limited for a meeting in Toledo in the morning.

(Nevertheless, Anderson exercised an option of the Madison Avenue speaker and took another couple of minutes to tell a final funny story that left the Sioux Room whooping with laughter and approval . . . a story so hilarious that would we

had room to include it.)

appendix b

handy 13-point tear-out check list for use in preparation of Madison Avenue speeches

	yes	no
1. have I determined the minimum length circumstances will permit my speech to be?	☐	☐
2. have I divided my speech into parts —one part for every three minutes, on the average, of talking time?	☐	☐
3. have I based each part upon a different subject, taking care only that each subject has specific interest for my audience?	☐	☐
4. have I devoted enough time to these subjects down by the old mill stream of consciousness, seining particularly for *facts* and *examples*?	☐	☐

5. have I wrung further material from all available intelligent minds . . . and perhaps even gotten one to write my whole speech? ☐ ☐

6. have I written my speech out word for word? ☐ ☐

7. have I ornamented my speech with a dozen or so examples from the various categories

  (funny stories
   visual aids
   audio aids
   demonstrations
   quotes
   literary nuggets
   homey sayings
   local grace notes
   attacks
   shocks
   vitalized statistics
   doctored clichés
   puns
   coined labels
   encapsulated summings up
   clarion calls to arms
   fables
   doggerel

    songs

    stunts

    question & answer periods)

of podium-proved accessories? □ □

8. have I used plenty of shortening and cut my speech down to its budgeted length? □ □

9. have I read my speech to a child (or other friend or relative) with a mental age of 12, and rewritten the muddy parts till they're clear as gin? □ □

10. have I rehearsed my speech till it seems entirely unrehearsed? □ □

11. have I vowed to talk and move *naturally* when I'm on? □ □

12. have I reviewed the pragmatic notes and, particularly . . . □ □

13. have I, come to think of it, a really good reason for suffering the indignity of being scared—and the nuisance of concealing it—in the first place? □ □